THE STORY OF CHEMISTRY

THE STORY OF CHEMISTRY

by Mae and Ira Freeman

illustrated by Charles Goslin

j540

THIS EDITION IS PRINTED AND DISTRIBUTED BY SPECIAL
ARRANGEMENT WITH THE ORIGINATORS AND PUBLISHERS,
Random House, Inc., NEW YORK, BY

E. M. HALE AND COMPANY
EAU CLAIRE, WISCONSIN

CONTENTS

1209556

THE STORY OF CHEMISTRY

THINGS ARE
MADE
OF MOLECULES

Have you ever seen a rocket rise into the sky? The fuel that sent it up was made by chemistry.

Did your doctor give you penicillin the last time you were sick? This helpful medicine was first found by a chemist.

Do you have a shirt or sweater or jacket made of nylon? The science of chemistry gave you this strong, lightweight material.

The story of chemistry is really the story of

all the different kinds of things in the world. If you want to know about chemistry, that means you want to know about what everything is made of.

All things are made of some kind of MATERIAL. A material is anything that takes up room. Look around you right now. See how many different kinds of material there are. Your chair is made of wood. The window is made of glass. Your mother's ring is made of gold.

There are hundreds of materials right in your room. Chemists work with thousands and thousands of others. The story of chemistry tells about materials. It tells how they can be changed and how new ones are made.

How would you try to find out what a piece of chalk is made of? You could crumble it into tiny pieces. But each little bit would still be only a piece of chalk. And you still would not know what chalk *really* is. It seems to be put together from tiny pieces of chalk! But what are those tiny pieces made of?

Now suppose you start to break the little

Everything is made of some kind of MATERIAL.

Smaller and smaller
bits of chalk. The smallest bits you
can get are called MOLECULES.

pieces of chalk into smaller and smaller bits. Suppose you could make them so small that nobody could see them, even with the strongest microscope. Each bit would be so tiny that there would have to be billions of them together before you could see even the littlest piece of chalk.

These tiny bits are called MOLECULES. They are molecules of chalk. They are the smallest specks of chalk you can have.

There are about a million other materials in the world. Each one is made up of its own special kind of molecule. Try to imagine how everything around you is made of molecules. Even a hard, smooth stone is really just a crowd of tiny specks.

MOLECULES ARE MADE OF ATOMS

Suppose you had some way of counting all the molecules in the head of a pin. Even if all the people in the United States helped you, it would take nearly 200 years to do it.

But there are things that are even smaller than molecules! Molecules themselves are made up of very tiny pieces called ATOMS. Each molecule is just a set of atoms joined together in its own special way. Some molecules have many atoms in them. If even one of these atoms is changed, the material becomes very different.

Think of any material. Suppose you choose water. All molecules of water are put together in a special way. Each one has just certain atoms in it. If any atom is changed, the material is not water any more. It becomes something else.

That is how it is for everything. Each material has molecules that are made of matching sets of atoms. You can be sure that no other material has the same set.

Atoms are not all alike. There are about a hundred different kinds of atoms. Each kind is called a chemical ELEMENT. Only chemists get to know most of the elements. But some

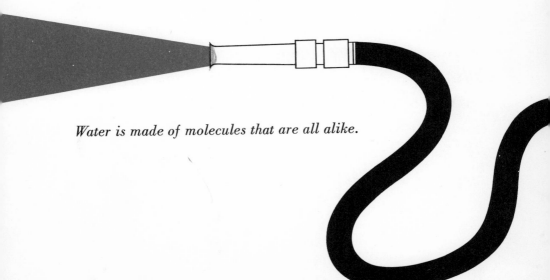

Water is made of molecules that are all alike.

are materials that everybody knows. Here are a few elements you may have seen:

Aluminum   Light, silvery metal. It is used for making pots, window screens, food wrappers.

Carbon   Black, smudgy material. Coal is mostly carbon. There is carbon in a pencil lead. Charcoal is carbon, too.

Copper   Soft, reddish metal. Electric wires are made of copper. There is copper in pennies.

Gold   Heavy, yellow metal. It is used in making jewelry.

Iron   Gray metal. It is used in making steel for buildings, ships, bridges, machines. Such things as nails, tools, and needles are made of iron or steel, too.

Silver   Heavy, white metal. It can be used for making jewelry, coins, knives, forks and spoons.

Tin   Silvery white metal. Most of it is used in making tin cans.

*Each of these things
has in it a chemical* ELEMENT
that you know.

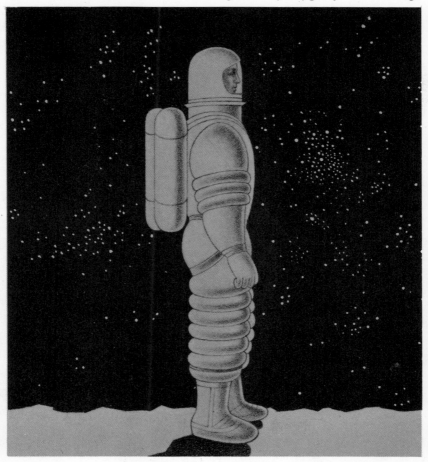

There is another element that you need all the time, but you have never seen it. It is called OXYGEN, and is in the air you breathe. It is one of the most important of all the elements.

HOW MOLECULES
ARE
PUT TOGETHER

Molecules are made by putting atoms together in different ways.

Some molecules have just *one kind* of atom in them. Then the material is an element. But some molecules have *different kinds* of atoms in them. Then the material is called a COMPOUND.

Water is a compound because it has two kinds of atoms in its molecules.

In every molecule of water there are

>2 atoms of HYDROGEN
>
>1 atom of OXYGEN

These atoms are not just mixed with each other. They are really *joined,* and stick together to make a molecule. Water is made of molecules like this. It takes billions and billions of them to make one drop of water.

Sugar is another compound. In each molecule of sugar there are

>12 atoms of CARBON
>
>22 atoms of HYDROGEN
>
>11 atoms of OXYGEN

They are hooked together as the drawing shows. Every sugar molecule is like this.

These are not real pictures of molecules. The drawings just show how atoms are joined to form molecules.

Vinegar is made up of molecules that have

>2 atoms of CARBON
>
>4 atoms of HYDROGEN
>
>2 atoms of OXYGEN

You can see that sugar and vinegar have the same kinds of atoms in them. But the numbers

A molecule of water

A molecule of sugar

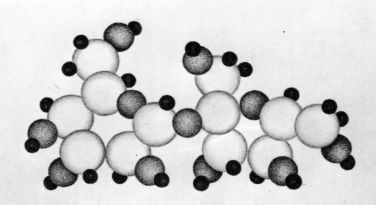

A molecule of vinegar

of atoms are not the same, and this makes a big difference in the material. Sugar is sweet and grainy. Vinegar is sour and watery.

These days, chemists can do many wonderful things with molecules. They can take atoms away from some molecules and join them to others. They can put together molecules that were never known before.

Chemists can make new kinds of cloth and new fuels for cars and jet planes. They can make new building materials, foods, and medicines. Now there are many plastics and other materials that were not even known just a few years ago. Later in this book you will find out about some of these things that make life better for all of us.

TELLING
MATERIALS
APART

It is easy to tell one animal from another by its shape or by the sound it makes. Some animals have smooth coats. Others are furry or woolly. One kind may bark and another kind may moo. Each kind of animal has special things about it that tell what it is.

Every material in chemistry has some things that are special about it, too.

That is how a chemist can tell each material from all the others. Each material has its own color, smell, taste, or form.

Chemists have another way to find out something about a material. They see what happens to it when it is put with other materials.

Everything that you can notice about a material is called a PROPERTY of the material. An onion has a special smell that tells you what it is. This smell is a property of onions. Sugar tastes sweet, and this is one of its properties.

It might happen that two materials have some properties that are alike. But their properties cannot *all* be alike. Otherwise they would really be the *same* material.

Water and glass are materials that you can see through. Both have this same property. But water is a LIQUID. It flows, and you can pour it from one dish to another. Glass is SOLID, and holds its shape. This difference is enough to show that water and glass are different materials.

Water has no color or smell. Oxygen has no color or smell, either. So these two materials have some properties that are alike. But we

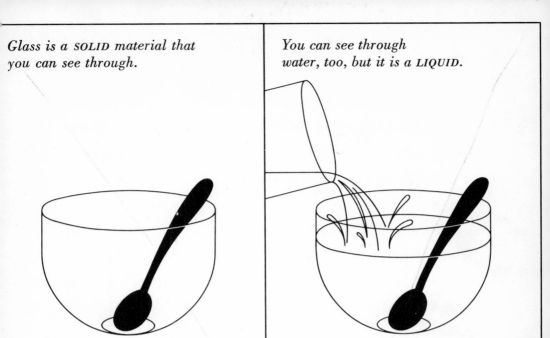

Glass is a SOLID material that you can see through.

You can see through water, too, but it is a LIQUID.

know they are different materials because water is a liquid and oxygen is a GAS.

A gas has no definite shape. It can drift around and spread out everywhere if it is not kept closed in.

A material can have the FORM of a solid, a liquid, or a gas. Form is one of the most important properties of a material.

Chemists have a list of the main properties of thousands and thousands of compounds. This helps them know the materials they find in their work.

Sometimes a chemist wants to separate two materials that are mixed together. He can do this if they are different in one of their properties. Here is an experiment that shows how this can be done.

Suppose you put some sugar and some sand in a small glass. Cover the glass and shake it well. You will see that the mixture is no longer white like sugar or brown like sand. It now looks tan or light yellow.

If you look closely, you can still see separate bits of sugar and sand.

Shake the sugar and sand to mix them.

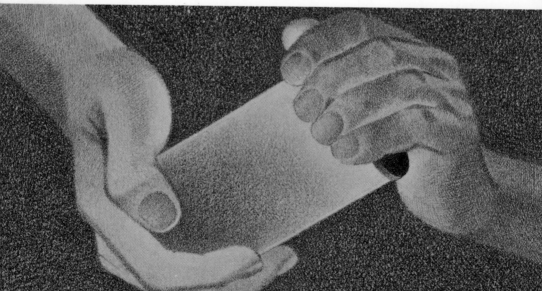

Suppose you want to separate the two materials again. It can be done. One way would be to spread the mixture out on a sheet of paper. Then you could push each grain of sand to one side with a needle. But this would take months! There is an easy way if you use a difference in the properties of sugar and sand.

Put some water into the mixture. Stir it for half a minute or so, and let it stand. Then carefully pour the water off into another glass. The sand stays behind, but you do not notice any sugar. It is really still there, in the water. Its molecules have separated from each other, and they are so tiny that you cannot see them.

When something breaks up so that its molecules spread through a liquid, it goes into SOLUTION. The sugar is in solution. Touch the tip of your finger to the liquid and then to your tongue. The sweet taste tells you that the sugar is still there, even if you cannot see it. It is spread all through the water, in the form of separate sugar molecules. That is what the solution is.

Now try to get the sugar back. Put the solution aside in a warm place for a day or two. When the water is all gone, you will see the sugar again. It is the white crust on the inside of the glass.

In the experiment, you found out how to separate two materials, sugar and sand. You could do it because of a difference in one of their properties. Sugar goes into solution in water, but sand does not.

CHEMICAL CHANGES

The experiment with sand and sugar showed that mixing things does not change the materials themselves. Each one was still there in the mixture. Each material kept its own properties all along. It was not hard to separate the two after they were mixed.

But chemists find that materials sometimes change so that you cannot get them back. This can happen with sugar. When candy is made, sugar is heated and it melts. It begins to bubble and turn brown. When this happens, the sugar molecules break down. The brown color is from carbon, which comes loose from the sugar molecules.

After the heat is turned off, the melted sugar becomes shiny and hard, like glass. It is a very different material from the white grains that were there at the start. That is because there has been a CHEMICAL CHANGE.

There was no chemical change when you made a solution of sugar in water. You found that you could get the white sugar back just by waiting for the water to dry away. The sugar molecules did not change.

But when sugar is cooked, the molecules themselves change. They break down into other kinds of molecules that have new properties. The sugar is gone for good.

After a chemical change, there is usually no easy way to get back what you had at the start. It is like trying to get back the milk, eggs, and flour after baking a cake!

You can do one or two experiments that show chemical changes. Put a teaspoonful of baking soda into a glass and then pour in a little vinegar. The bubbling and foaming show that some kind of gas is formed. Where did it come from? It formed from the molecules of the materials you mixed. Putting the two materials together caused a chemical change. The molecules that are left in the liquid afterward are different from what they were before.

Make a chemical change by mixing vinegar and baking soda.

Put three or four drops of writing ink into about half an inch of water in a glass. Stir the solution well. Then pour in a spoonful of laundry bleach and stir again. The blue liquid loses its color as if by magic. There has been a chemical change. The blue coloring in the ink has been changed to a material that has no color.

Hundreds of chemical changes happen all around you all the time. Cream turns sour. Paint dries. Iron rusts. Bananas get ripe. Plants grow by taking materials from the ground and from the air.

Chemical changes go on in the kitchen, in the garden, in factories, and even inside *you*.

HOW CHEMISTRY GREW

A very long time ago, people knew nothing about chemistry. They were using some chemical changes without really knowing what was going on. They made fires for cooking, but they did not know what made fire burn.

Later they found out that when certain rocks were heated, shiny metals would come out. They believed this was some kind of magic and did not think further about it.

As time went on, some people began to

wonder about such things and started to ask questions. One group had the idea that all the materials in the world were mixtures of just four things—earth, air, fire, and water. But they did not do experiments to test this idea, and so they did not get very far.

There were other people who did experiments, but they had one main interest. They tried to make gold out of ordinary metals such as iron. In almost every country, the king would put men to work on this problem. They tried to find some secret way of making gold. These men were called ALCHEMISTS.

For hundreds of years the work went on. Each king wanted to find a way to make gold. He knew his kingdom would then become the most powerful in the world. But it never worked. No alchemist ever found a way to make the magic change.

The alchemists worked in dark and stuffy rooms that were full of smoke and bad smells. They used all sorts of queer materials that they heated in pots over open fires. Sometimes, one of them would pretend he had found a

way to make gold. When the truth came out, he would be thrown out of the country or put to death.

After a time, people began to think about other things than making gold. Somebody found how to make vinegar out of wood. Others learned how to make dyes and to work with metals. Slowly, the science of chemistry grew.

One of the things chemists wondered about was: "What happens when something burns?" They had the idea that a mysterious material came out of every burning object. This seemed to be true, because whenever wood or paper burns, only a little ash is left.

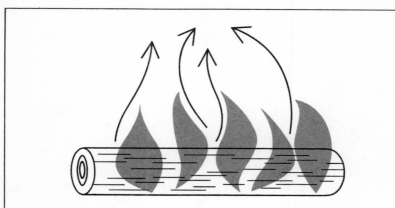

When something burns, it joins up with oxygen in the air.

Then, about the time George Washington lived, chemists discovered what really happens. Whenever anything burns, it joins up chemically with oxygen from the air. This makes new compounds that are mostly gases, which get away. That is why there seems to be almost nothing left afterward.

To test this idea, chemists burned some things in a closed box. There was air in the box, too. They weighed the closed box carefully before and after the burning. It weighed exactly the same both times! This showed that nothing inside the box was really used up.

Next, they punched a hole in the side of the box. As they did this, they heard air rush in. The burning material had grabbed up oxygen from the air that was in the box at the start. That made room for more air to go in.

Now chemists knew exactly what happens when things burn. The burning material joins up chemically with oxygen.

You can see why oxygen is such an important element. Oxygen is used by all animals that breathe. Breathing is like a slow kind of burning. The fuel is the food you eat. You get energy for everything you do when this fuel joins with oxygen in your body.

In the last few years, chemistry has gone ahead faster than ever before. Chemists can do wonderful things with well-known materials. They are able to make many new materials, too. They do not try to make great lumps of gold, but they are finding far greater treasures than the alchemists ever dreamed of.

IRON

AND STEEL

When you think of chemistry, perhaps you think of scientists working in a quiet room. You may imagine them mixing liquids in a glass or heating materials over a flame.

But not all chemical work is like this. Very important chemical changes go on in a hot, smoky, noisy steel mill. That is the place where iron is changed into steel. And instead of a small glass of material, huge piles of iron and coal are used.

Even if you are miles away, you know the steel mill is there. It is a noisy place. You can see great clouds of smoke from the tall chimneys. At night, flames from the furnaces light up the sky.

Iron is a metal that comes from the earth. Some metals are found in the rocks as shiny little lumps, but iron does not come this way. You do not see the iron at all because it is part of a reddish-brown sandy material called iron ORE.

Iron ore is a compound of iron atoms joined to oxygen atoms. This compound is found in the ground in some places. After it is dug up, the ore goes to the steel mill. That is where the oxygen is taken away from the iron.

Oxygen atoms hold iron atoms very tightly. To make the oxygen let go of the iron, carbon is put in with the iron ore. Then the mixture is placed in a BLAST FURNACE and made very hot. The carbon atoms grab the oxygen, and the iron is left all by itself as iron metal.

The iron is so hot that it is a liquid. It gathers in drops and falls to the bottom of the blast furnace. Every few hours, the liquid iron is run out. Most of it is taken away in special cars to another part of the mill, where it will be changed to steel. Some of the melted iron is left to get hard and form huge blocks.

The iron that comes from the blast furnace usually has some carbon left in it. This kind of iron is good for making sinks and pipes, but it cracks and breaks too easily for many other uses. That is because there is too much carbon in it.

To make the iron stronger, most of the carbon must be taken out. The liquid iron is put into big pots and air is pumped through it. The oxygen in the air hooks up with the carbon and burns it away. When this happens, giant flames shoot up a hundred feet high and there is a great shower of sparks. After everything is finished, the iron has been changed into STEEL. Steel is iron with only a little carbon left in it.

There are many kinds of steel for different uses. Chemists are always watching over it while it is being made. From time to time

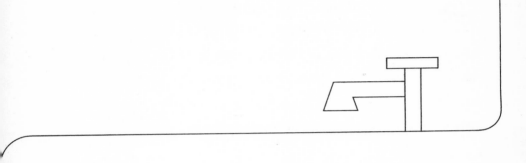

Sinks and pipes can be made of iron.

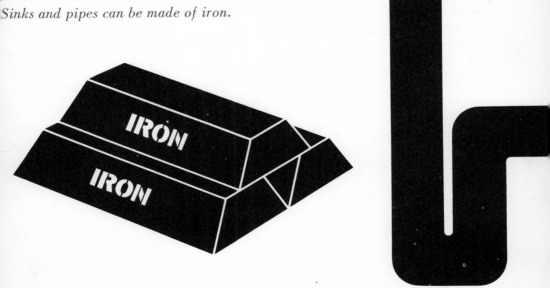

they take off samples and test them. Then they can tell the steel man what to do to make special kinds of steel. They know how to do this by adding little bits of other metals.

Some steel must be extra strong for making frames and bars that are used in ships, buildings, and bridges. Other kinds of steel are needed for making wire, tools, or automobiles. A very special kind is used for making the magnets of huge atom smashers.

In the kitchen you find knives, forks, and spoons of STAINLESS STEEL. This metal does not rust easily or become eaten away by chemicals.

There are very many uses for different kinds of steel. And the chemist is the one who finds out how each kind should be made.

MORE

ABOUT METALS

Long before people worked with iron, they knew about another metal. It is the reddish metal called COPPER. Copper is a chemical element, just as iron is. But copper is sometimes found all by itself, and not joined to other elements.

When the earth was young, part of the rock deep down in the ground was so hot that it was liquid. The melted rock often had copper in it. Now and then, some of this rock flowed out. It cooled off and became solid. Little by little, water wore the rock away and small lumps of copper were left behind.

People in many parts of the world began to use this metal. It was found in China, in Africa, and in America. American Indians knew about copper long before the white man came. They found that these strange reddish lumps could be hammered into many shapes. They made tools, fishhooks, and jewelry out of copper. Later, the Indians found they could melt this metal and shape it into cups and dishes.

American Indians made useful things of copper.

Copper ore is often dug out of the side of a mountain.

Copper is a useful metal these days, and very much of it is needed. The little bits found in rocks are not enough. There is much more copper in the ground, but it is joined with other materials. It is in compounds called copper ore.

In some places, whole mountains are dug away to get copper ore out. The ore must be crushed and washed. Then it is roasted to get the metal out. But the copper is still not very pure. It has bits of other metals in it, and they must be taken away. Electricity is used to do this. Sheets of copper are put into big tanks full of a chemical solution. Then electricity is sent through the liquid. This makes the copper come out as pure copper metal.

The other materials drop to the bottom of the tank. They are saved because they have valuable metals in them, such as silver and gold!

Copper metal has many uses. Of all the copper taken from the earth, nearly half is made into electric wires. That is because this metal can carry electricity better than almost

Electricity is used to make sheets of copper pure.

any other material.

There are so many copper parts in a car that they weigh almost as much as you do. At home, you may have copper pots in the kitchen, copper water pipes, and copper window screens.

Many of our most useful metals are mixtures. Copper can be melted together with other metals to make BRONZE or BRASS. Most gold jewelry has some copper in it. Gold itself is too soft for making rings and pins. Adding copper makes it stronger.

In nearly every country, some of the small coins have copper in them to make them last longer. A penny is almost all copper, as you can tell from its color. But you would never guess that there is copper in nickels, dimes, quarters, and half dollars.

Compounds of copper are used in making such things as insect killers, paints, electric batteries, and dyes for cloth.

Besides iron and copper, there are other important metals. ALUMINUM is one of them. This metal is never found by itself, but only in compounds. Clay is a compound that has aluminum in it.

People did not know about aluminum for a long time. That is because it was so hard to get this metal all by itself. At last, about 75 years ago, a bright young American chemist found a way to do it. He used electricity to make aluminum come out of its compounds.

One thing that makes aluminum metal so useful is its lightness. It is much lighter than steel but can be made nearly as strong. To make it strong, aluminum must be mixed with small amounts of other metals. Then it can be used for building airplanes, cars, trains, and even the sides of houses.

Aluminum has another good property. It can protect itself from the weather. It does this by joining with oxygen from the air. This forms a coating that covers the metal and sticks to it.

In this way, aluminum is better than iron. Iron hooks up with oxygen from the air, too. But the iron forms rust, which does not stick. It crumbles off, and after a while the whole piece of iron may rust away.

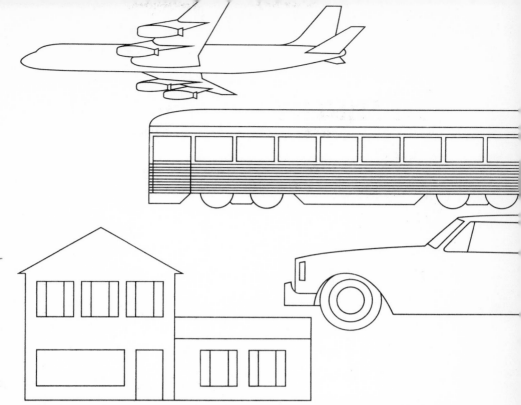

Planes, trains, cars, and even houses can be made of aluminum.

In your home, you can see aluminum in many forms. There may be pots and pans made of this metal. There is aluminum foil for wrapping food to keep air out. Many parts of a washing machine or a vacuum cleaner are aluminum. Even paint is made of this metal. So are tubes for tooth paste. There seems to be no end to what this light and strong metal can do.

CHEMISTRY

AND

OIL

Suppose someone asked you to name the most useful and valuable liquid in the world. You would have to say, "Water." No animal or plant can live without this liquid.

There is another liquid that is almost as important as water. It is a thick, bad-smelling, oily material found in the ground. It is called PETROLEUM. No machine or engine could run without petroleum and the things we get from it.

Tall towers are used in drilling into the ground for oil.

Until a hundred years ago, all buildings were lit by candles or by lamps that burned whale oil. Abraham Lincoln read his books by the light of an open fire. Petroleum had already been used in lamps, but there was not much of it. Then people found a way to drill deep holes in the ground. This made it easy to get petroleum in large amounts. Sometimes it rushed out of the hole in great streams. Soon oil wells were being drilled in many places.

Petroleum is a mixture of many materials. These must be separated from each other for different uses. Chemists have a way of doing this by heating the petroleum in large tanks. This makes different liquids come out of the mixture, one after another. First come the light, watery ones. Next, there are heavier oils. Then there are thick, sticky ones. The last to come out are the heaviest and thickest of all.

One of the thinner mixtures that comes out of petroleum is a clear liquid called gasoline. For about 50 years, nobody knew what to do with this liquid. It was thrown away! Then automobiles began to be used, and gasoline became one of the most important parts of petroleum.

These days, every liquid that comes from petroleum is saved to make useful things. Some of them are shown in the picture on the next page. Things that use the light parts of petroleum are near the top of the picture. Those that use the heavy parts are toward the bottom. There are hundreds of others.

Chemists had to find out more about petroleum before they could make all these things. They learned that petroleum is a mixture of

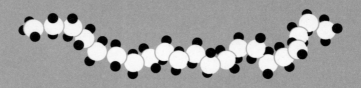

nearly 60 compounds called HYDROCARBONS.

The pictures on page 15 showed how the atoms are hooked together in a molecule of water or a molecule of sugar. In hydrocarbons, carbon atoms are joined together in a special way. They form a chain. There are also hydrogen atoms hooked on along the sides, as in the drawings on this page. That is why these molecules are called hydrocarbons.

Each mixture that comes from petroleum has hydrocarbons of different lengths in it. Gasoline is a mixture of hydrocarbons that have between 6 and 10 carbon atoms in their chains. This is how they are made up:

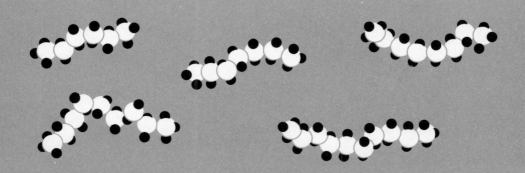

There are hydrocarbons with shorter chains in some fuels used for cooking. There are some with longer chains in machine oils. Paraffin wax and asphalt are made of molecules with very long chains.

Every year people use more cars, trucks, and airplanes. Chemists had to think of ways to get more gasoline. They found out how to hook shorter hydrocarbons together to make chains that were the right length. They also found out how to break up longer chains into molecules for gasoline. Besides this, chemists found ways of getting some hydrocarbons from coal.

Later in this book you will see how they can turn hydrocarbons into plastics, dyes, medicines, and many other things.

CHEMISTRY
AND
FOOD

Useful chemical changes go on all the time in many places all over the world. But some of the most important chemical changes of all are the ones that go on inside *you*. Every person is a natural chemical factory. So is every animal and plant. Your food goes through many chemical changes after you eat it.

Your body is like an engine in some ways. An engine will not work well unless it has the right kind of fuel, such as coal or gasoline.

Engines need fuel to run machines. In the same way, food is the fuel that you need for work and play and everything you do.

Food does more than just keep the body going. It makes it grow. It builds up parts of the body. Food keeps you alive and healthy.

Food chemists found that there are different groups of materials that we must eat to stay active and well. One of these groups is made up of sugar and starch. Both sugar and starch have only carbon, oxygen, and hydrogen in them. Chemists call them CARBOHYDRATES. There are carbohydrates in the well-known foods shown in the pictures on this page and the next.

maple syrup

SUGA

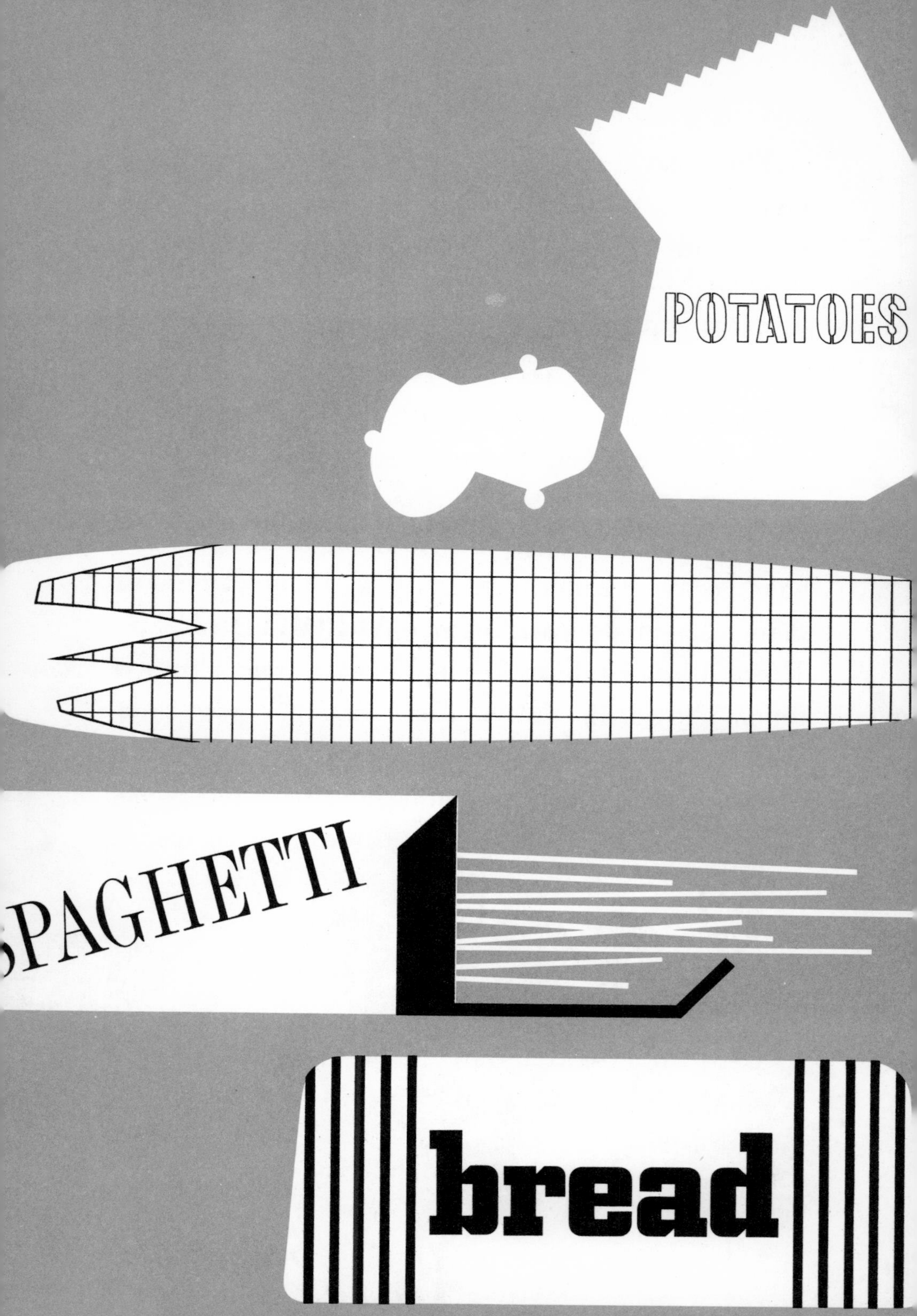

POTATOES

SPAGHETTI

bread

The starch in your food cannot be used the way it comes. First your body has to change the starch chemically to a kind of sugar. Then this sugar can be taken up and used.

You get most of your energy from starch and sugar. That is why most of the food you eat is made up of these compounds. But if you get more starch and sugar than your body can use, the rest is changed to fat.

Chemists have a way of testing things to see if they have starch in them. You can make this test on some of the foods in the picture. You will need a small bottle of iodine solution from the drug store. There may be one in your first-aid kit at home.

Get a small tin can and put two tablespoons of water into it. Then put in a few drops of the iodine and stir with a small stick. Iodine can make bad stains. Do not get any on your skin or clothes, and *never* get any near your mouth.

Use the stick to put a few drops of the testing solution on a piece of white bread. The bread turns dark blue wherever the solution touches it. This color tells you that there is starch in bread. Anything that has starch in it will turn blue when iodine is put on it.

Try the test on some other foods, too. Try small pieces of apple, spaghetti, cheese, and banana to see if you get the blue color. Throw away the pieces of food, the can, and the stick just as soon as you have finished your tests.

Starch and sugar give you energy to keep you going. There are some other food materials that do this, too. These are FATS, which come mostly from butter, fish, meat, and cooking oils. The body uses fats as a fuel. Fats also help by carrying some of the chemicals you need to different parts of the body.

LARD

Cooking Oil

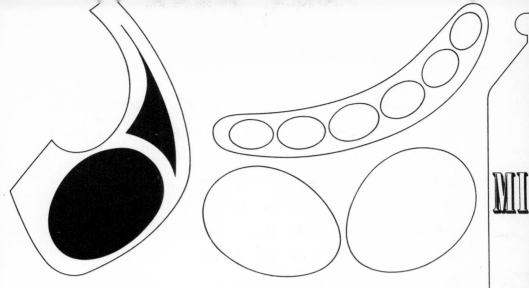

Another important kind of food material is called PROTEIN. Proteins are very big molecules, made up of hundreds of atoms. There are carbon, hydrogen, oxygen, nitrogen, and sulfur atoms in these giant molecules.

Proteins are the building foods that help you grow. Each part of your body is made up of tiny blobs called CELLS. There are always some cells that are wearing out, and proteins help build new ones to take their place. The picture shows some of the best protein foods.

MINERALS make up another group of foods that everybody needs. Some of the main mineral compounds have iron, calcium, and phosphorus in them. They help grow strong bones and teeth. They build muscles and blood.

As plants grow, they take up minerals from the ground. You get these compounds when you eat fruits and vegetables. You get minerals from milk, meat, and fish, too.

There is something else that is found in everything you eat. It is one of the most important materials of all. It is water. More than half of your body is water.

Some foods have very much water in them. You cannot see it, but there is a whole glass of water in each loaf of bread. A hamburger looks like solid meat, but half of it is really water. There are about three glasses of water in every quart of ice cream. But you need even more water than this. Doctors say you should drink about six glasses of water each day.

It is possible to eat good food and still not stay healthy. Doctors used to wonder about this. Starch and sugar, fats, proteins, and minerals sometimes did not seem to be enough.

Then, after years of hard work, chemists found some new compounds that all people need in their food. They called these com-

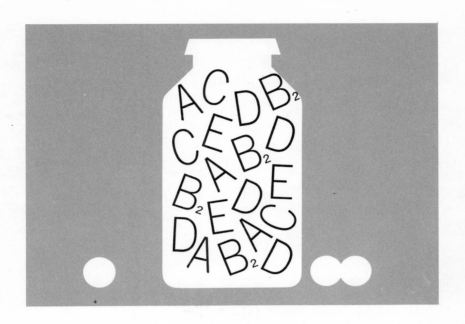

pounds VITAMINS. There are about 20 different kinds of vitamins. Some of them give you energy and others help you eat more. There are also vitamins that protect your body against sickness.

Vitamins are found in very tiny amounts in most foods, but some people do not get enough vitamins this way. Luckily, many of these compounds can be made by chemists. Now doctors can give people vitamin pills to help out.

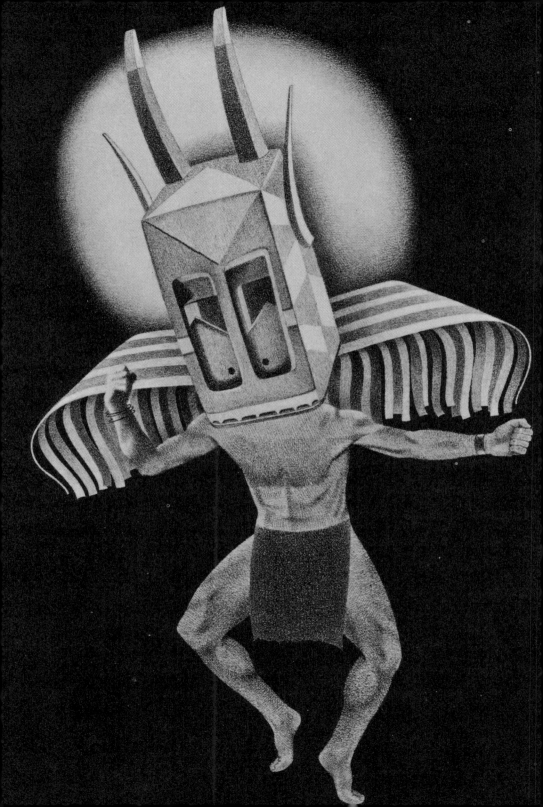

WONDER
DRUGS

Long ago, people thought that all sickness was caused by evil spirits. Wild tribes had witch doctors who tried to drive away the evil spirits by dancing or making loud noises.

When the alchemists saw they could not make gold, they began trying to make all kinds of queer medicines. They even used such strange materials as chopped-up worms and onions. Of course, none of their drugs worked. Now we have many wonder drugs that cure sick people and save many lives. Chemists and other scientists found how to make these drugs just in the last few years.

Even in Abraham Lincoln's time, people did not know that most sickness is caused by GERMS. Germs are very tiny plants and animals. They are everywhere. Some of them are too small to see, even with a microscope.

Not all germs are bad. There are useful ones that we could not get along without. Some make plants grow. Others help by making chemical changes in the food that animals eat. All germs do their work by causing chemical changes.

Some germ-killing chemicals are used on the outside of the body. In a first-aid kit you usually find iodine, mercurochrome, or other such chemicals. You can put one of these on a cut finger. It will keep harmful germs from getting in and making trouble.

About fifty years ago, a scientist first found that chemicals could also kill germs *inside* the body. Then, not long ago, chemists were able to make a group of materials called SULFA drugs.

The sulfa compounds can cure many kinds of sickness. They save thousands of lives every year. Sulfa drugs do not really kill germs, but only weaken them. Then the chemicals in the body can attack these germs and kill them off.

There are some kinds of germs that the sulfa drugs cannot work against. Luckily, scientists were able to find other chemical germ-fighters to help out. They found one of them in a very unusual way.

Did you ever see an old piece of bread that had some fuzzy green and yellow spots on it? These spots are made up of tiny plants called MOLDS. An English scientist was using some dangerous germs in his experiments. These germs were growing in glass dishes.

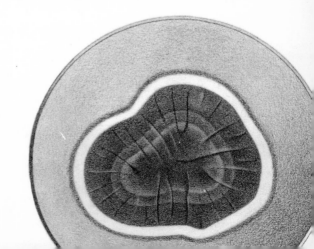

A mold found on a glass dish gave chemists a wonder drug.

One day, the scientist noticed a spot of mold in one of the dishes. He started to throw the spoiled dish away. But suddenly he saw something unusual. There was a clear ring all around the spot of mold, and no germs were growing there. He knew there must be something in that blue-green mold that could fight germs.

After much work, the scientist found what it was. The mold was able to make tiny amounts of a germ-killing chemical. He named it PENICILLIN. This new chemical worked against some germs that the sulfa drugs could not fight. Now penicillin is made in huge steel tanks. Drug stores and hospitals keep some of it ready for use all the time.

Soon more wonder drugs were found. Most of them come from the soil. Scientists had to make thousands of tests to find them. Now there are many kinds, such as STREPTOMYCIN, TERRAMYCIN, and others. Each one is good for fighting certain germs.

Chemists were able to work out how the molecules of these drugs are put together. And

Penicillin is now made in huge steel tanks.

now they do not have to get all these compounds from the soil. They just make some of them from other chemicals.

In the past, there were no cures for many kinds of sickness. These days, it is wonderful to have sulfa drugs, penicillin, and other such helpful medicines. It is quite right to call them "wonder drugs."

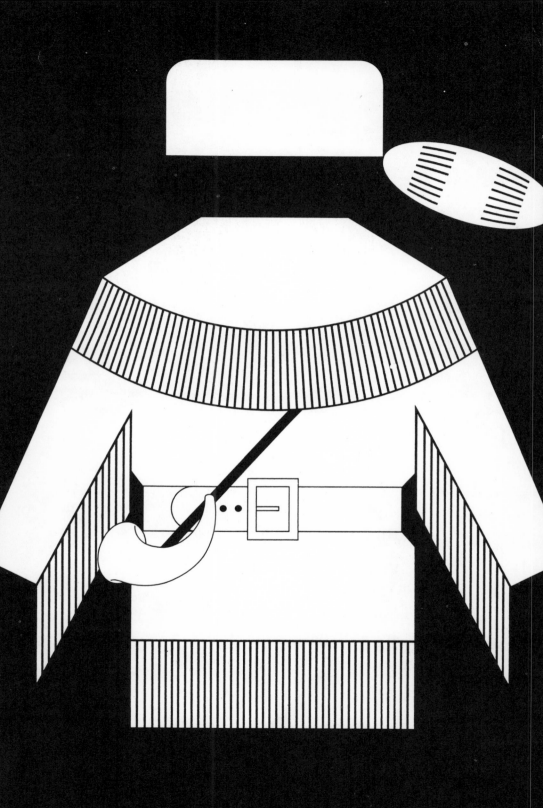

PLASTICS

In times long past, clothes were made from the skins of animals. Cave men dressed in the fur of bears or mountain lions. Daniel Boone wore a buckskin jacket.

Then people learned how to make thread out of FIBERS of plants. A fiber is a long, thin strip of any material. People used fibers of grass, wool, silk, or cotton, and wove them into cloth. Then they put pieces of cloth together and made clothing.

It was not always easy to find enough fibers of the right kind for making cloth. Then, not many years ago, chemists learned how to make fibers out of chemicals. They got these chemicals from coal, gas, wood, petroleum, and even milk.

These days, you wear things made of fibers that never grew on any plant or animal. Instead, they come from chemicals made in a factory.

One of the new fibers is called RAYON. It is made by grinding up wood and mixing it with some chemicals. It becomes a sticky liquid. Then it is forced through tiny holes into a special solution. This makes each stream

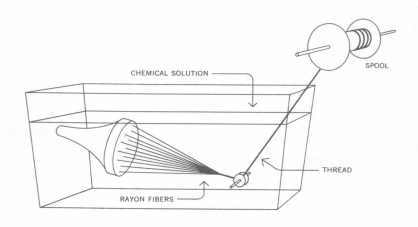

CHEMICAL SOLUTION

SPOOL

THREAD

RAYON FIBERS

of the liquid become hard and form a fiber. The fibers are twisted into threads for weaving rayon cloth.

Instead of forcing the liquid through holes, it can be made into thin sheets. You know it by the name of CELLOPHANE. It is used to wrap food, candy, gifts, and many other things.

There is another very useful kind of fiber called NYLON. It is made out of chemicals that come from coal, air, and water. Each nylon molecule is a long chain of hundreds of hydrogen, oxygen, carbon, and nitrogen atoms. The fibers can be made into clothing, fishing lines, brushes, and all kinds of things that you use every day.

Chemists made some other fiber materials that are like nylon. They have names such as ORLON, SARAN, and DACRON. Each one has its special uses.

Another kind of fiber comes from skim milk. This fiber is like wool. It is even better than natural wool from sheep.

All the fiber materials you have just read

about are really PLASTICS. A plastic is any soft material that will keep its shape after it is set.

Chemists have been able to make many plastics. Some are clear, like glass. Others can be made in any color. Some are stiff and hard, but others can be bent. No matter which plastic he is making, a chemist starts with small molecules. He hooks them together in different ways to make very big molecules.

The picture shows a few of the things made from plastics. Many of these used to be formed from metals. Now they are made of these new materials that are so bright and clean and easy to use.

MORE WAYS
THAT CHEMISTRY
HELPS PEOPLE

Chemicals are a great help on the farm. The farmer must have FERTILIZERS for his crops. Fertilizers are chemicals that plants need in order to grow. Chemists add vitamins to animal food to make it better. Chemicals such as DDT help get rid of insects that harm plants.

Chemists have found ways of making many new kinds of paint. Paint is usually oil with coloring material in it. Now there are paints made of plastic, which protect things from the

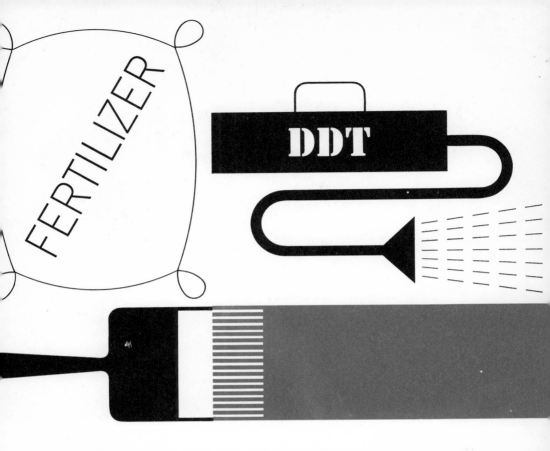

weather. There are others that use water in place of oil. They dry quickly and have no bad smell. There is also a kind of paint that keeps wood safe from fire.

Every time you take a picture you are using chemistry. The film has silver compounds on it. These compounds change when light hits them. Light comes into your camera from the outside and puts the picture on the film. This picture shows up when the film is developed

in chemical solutions.

Soap is made by melting fat with chemicals in huge tanks. In a soap factory, each tank may be as big as a swimming pool. The soap is shaped into cakes and left to get hard. For house cleaning and washing clothes, there are DETERGENTS. A detergent is a kind of soap that is made with petroleum oil instead of fat.

The atoms of some materials can be split apart to give great power. Big cities can get electricity from this power. It is also used to drive ships and submarines. Chemists work on the materials to make them pure so that their atoms can be split.

Without chemistry, no rocket or satellite could be shot into the sky. The fuel that drives a rocket up is made of special chemicals. Also, chemists had to make new kinds of materials to protect parts of the rocket from great heat. So even space travel cannot get along without chemistry.

SOME WORDS OF SCIENCE USED IN THIS BOOK

MATERIAL. *Everything that takes up room is made of some kind of material.*

CHEMISTRY. *The science of all the different kinds of materials in the world.*

SOLID, LIQUID, GAS. *The three forms that materials can have. A solid keeps its shape. A liquid flows. A gas drifts around.*

MOLECULES. *Tiny bits that make up all materials. There are about a million kinds of molecules in the world.*

ATOMS. *Parts of molecules. There are only about 100 different kinds of atoms.*

ELEMENT. *A material made of just one kind of atom. Iron, copper, and tin are elements.*

COMPOUND. *A material that has more than one kind of atom in its molecules.*

PROPERTIES. *The things you can notice about a material. They help you tell one material from another.*

CHEMICAL CHANGE. *Any change in the molecules of a material.*

SOLUTION. *Some materials break up into separate molecules when they are put into a liquid. Then the material is in solution.*

INDEX

The Authors

Mae and Ira Freeman are experts in bringing science to the public and especially to young people. Their other Easy-to-Read science books are *Your Wonderful World of Science; The Sun, the Moon, and the Stars; The Story of the Atom;* and *The Story of Electricity.*

Ira Freeman, Professor of Physics at Rutgers University, is the co-author with Arthur March of *The New World of Physics.*

The Artist

Charles Goslin has designed book jackets, record jackets, a magazine, and a United States postage stamp. He holds a Bachelor of Fine Arts degree from the Rhode Island School of Design. He and his wife live in Brooklyn, N.Y.

The Random House Easy-to-Read Science Library

Your Wonderful World of Science   *by Mae and Ira Freeman*

Rocks All Around Us   *by Anne Terry White*

The Sun, the Moon, and the Stars   *by Mae and Ira Freeman*

In the Days of the Dinosaurs   *by Roy Chapman Andrews*

Simple Machines and How They Work   *by Elizabeth N. Sharp*

Rockets Into Space   *by Alexander L. Crosby and Nancy Larrick*

The Story of the Atom   *by Mae and Ira Freeman*

Hurricanes, Tornadoes, and Blizzards   *by Kathryn Hitte*

Satellites in Outer Space   *by Isaac Asimov*

The Story of Numbers   *by Patricia Lauber*

Danger! Icebergs Ahead!   *by Lynn and Gray Poole*

The Story of Electricity   *by Mae and Ira Freeman*

Your Body and How It Works   *by Patricia Lauber*

The Story of Chemistry   *by Mae and Ira Freeman*